FLY GUY PRESENTS:

SHARKS

Tedd Arnold

Scholastic Inc.

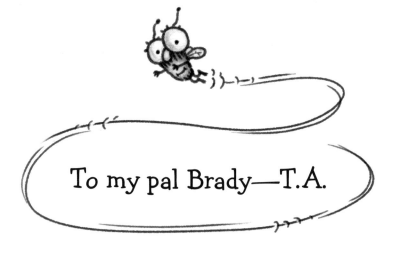

To my pal Brady—T.A.

Photos ©: cover: Stephen Frink/Getty Images; back cover: Bill Curtsinger/National Geographic Creative; 4–5: Audubon Nature Institute; 6 top: strmko/Getty Images; 6 center: FAUP/Shutterstock, Inc.; 6 bottom: divejunkie/Getty Images; 7 top left: Ginet-Drin/age fotostock; 7 top right: Dan Burton/age fotostock; 7 center: Seapics.com; 7 bottom: W. Scott/Shutterstock, Inc.; 8–9, 9 inset: Seapics.com; 10: Carlos Villoch/age fotostock; 11 top: Jim Agronick/Shutterstock, Inc.; 11 bottom, 12 top, 12 bottom: Seapics.com; 13 top: Andy Murch/Vwpics/Newscom; 13 bottom: MP cz/Shutterstock, Inc.; 14–15: Willyam Bradberry/Shutterstock, Inc.; 16: Tammy616/Getty Images; 17 top: Bill Curtsinger/National Geographic Creative; 17 bottom: Jurgen Freund/NPL/Minden Pictures; 18 top: Dray van Beeck/Shutterstock, Inc.; 18 bottom: Seapics.com; 19 top: demarfa/Getty Images; 19 center, bottom: Seapics.com; 20–21: Lawrence Cruciana/Shutterstock, Inc.; 20 inset: Seapics.com; 21 bottom: troischats/Getty Images; 22 top, bottom: Seapics.com; 23: Reinhard Dirscherl/age fotostock; 24–25: Marevision/age fotostock; 24 inset: Stuart Keasley/age fotostock; 26–27: ullstein bild/Getty Images; 28 top: David Doubilet/National Geographic Creative; 28 bottom: Yasumasa Kobayashi/Nature Production/Minden Pictures; 29 top: Jason Edwards/National Geographic Creative; 29 bottom: Doug Perrine/Nature Picture Library; 30 top: Norbert Probst/imageb/age fotostock; 30 bottom: Seapics.com; 31: Bill Curtsinger/National Geographic Creative.

ISBN 978-0-545-50771-4

36 35   23 24/0

Printed in the U.S.A.   40
First printing, January 2013

A boy had a pet fly named Fly Guy.
Fly Guy could say the boy's name —

Buzz and Fly Guy were at the
aquarium (ah-KWEAR-ee-um).

"Let's go see the sharks!" said Buzz.

Fly Guy seemed scared.

"Sharks are cool!" said Buzz.
"There's nothing to be afraid of
here at the aquarium."

They dived in to find out more....

Scientists have found about 400 different kinds of sharks. Each shark has amazing abilities.

GRAY REEF SHARK

BLUE SHARK

LEOPARD SHARK

Sharks are fish. They live in bodies of water all over the world—even in lakes and rivers!

Like other fish, sharks breathe through gills.

A shark's skeleton is made of cartilage (KAR-tuh-lij). Sharks don't have any bones.

great white shark

Cartilage makes sharks flexible. They can turn quickly to catch a bite to eat.

coral catshark

Sharks have many rows of teeth.
Only the front row is used for eating.

JAW OF A
NURSE SHARK

COOKIE-CUTTER
SHARK JAWS

The mouth of a shark can hold thousands of teeth at one time!

JAWS OF A
SAND TIGER SHARK

SAND TIGER
SHARK

Most sharks are carnivores (KAR-nih-vorz). They eat meat, such as fish and seagulls.

WHITETIP REEF SHARK

A shark uses its sharp teeth to rip its prey. Then the shark swallows the meat whole—without even chewing!

Not all sharks eat meat.

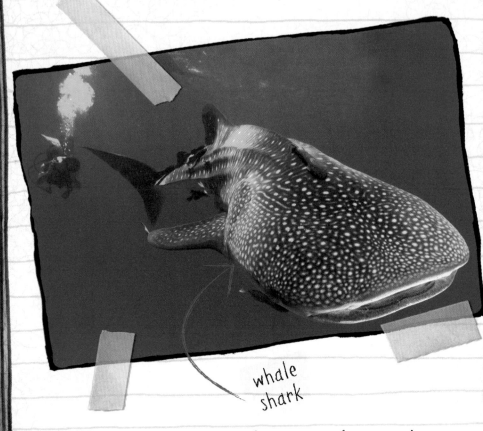

whale
shark

The whale shark is the largest shark in the world. It eats a small plant called plankton and other tiny plants.

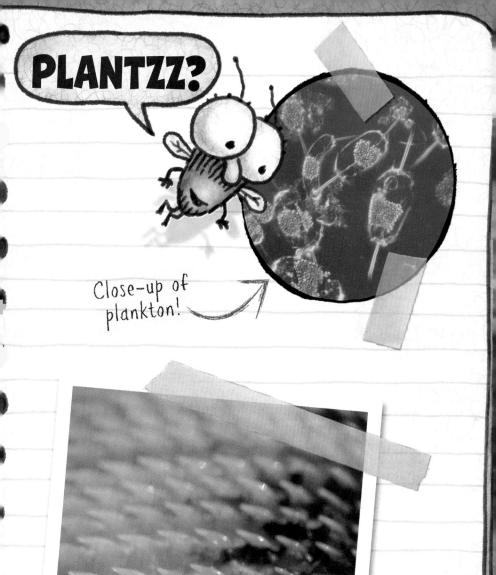

Close-up of plankton!

Close-up of whale-shark teeth!

Most sharks have rough skin made of denticles (DEN-tih-kuhlz).

BLUE SHARK

A BLUE SHARK'S TINY DENTICLES

It feels hard and sharp. Denticles protect sharks from harm.

GREAT WHITE SHARK

ROUGH AND TOUGH!

A GREAT WHITE SHARK'S DENTICLES

A GREENLAND SHARK'S DENTICLES

NURSE SHARK ○ ○ ○ ○ ○

Nurse sharks have smoother skin than most sharks. It feels like sandpaper.

Other fish have smooth, slippery scales. A shark's teeth can bite right through them.

Sharks have super senses. That makes them great hunters.

nose

Moses smoothhound shark

ear

Bigeye houndshark

A shark can hear its prey moving underwater! It can even hear a fish's muscles moving as it swims.

whitetip reef shark

A shark has special eyesight that helps it to navigate (NAV-ih-gayt) through dark, murky water.

Sharks are very smart. They have brains—just like humans and flies.

They have supersensitive noses to sniff out their next meal. Two-thirds of a shark's brain is used for smelling.

Many baby sharks, which are called pups, hatch from eggs. A mother shark can have up to 100 pups at a time.

A swell shark embryo within the egg.

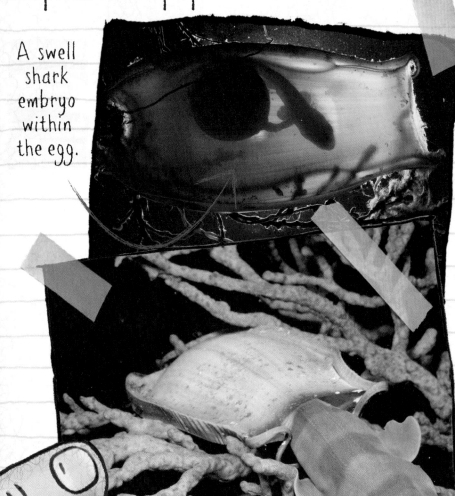

A newborn swell shark coming out of its egg case.

PUPPIEZZ

A newborn shark pup resting!

Most sharks live to be about 25 years old. That's way longer than the life of a fly!

A newborn lemon shark pup swimming away from its mother.

Sharks do not sleep. Most have to keep moving in order to breathe!

WHITETIP REEF SHARK

Sharks are superfast swimmers. They can move at up to 25 miles per hour! But they cannot swim backward.

GOBLIN SHARK

Some sharks are nocturnal (nok-TUR-nuhl) hunters. They are more active at night.

In the dark, a cookie-cutter shark uses a special light called luminescence (loo-mih-NEH-suhns). This light makes the shark look smaller so that its prey is not scared away. The shark surprises its prey and takes a cookie-sized bite!

COOKIE-CUTTER SHARK

This one glows in the dark!

"Wow!" said Buzz. "We learned a lot about sharks today. They are so cool!"

Fly Guy was not scared anymore.

"Fly Guy," said Buzz, "I can't wait for our next field trip!"